A Mother's Ramblings, Introspections, Learnings

Geeta Harisinganey

Presentation by *BookLeaf Publishing*

Web: www.bookleafpub.com

E-mail: info@bookleafpub.com

ISBN: 9789360942069

First edition 2024

I would like to dedicate the book to my daughter, Tarannum

My Journey with you my child is the most precious gift that life has bestowed on me. These poems are my guiding thoughts that helped me embrace my role of a mother and respect you as your own unique being. On this journey I have found you to be my teacher who has helped me to mature into a better version of me. I can't thank you enough, my child, for sharing this journey with me!

Epiphany

The nightmare shook my reverie
The failing dreams, the crumbling plans
Lost in my fractured thoughts, what if...
I dare not....but you caught on
What if...You had never encountered me?
A glistening tear threatened to fall
And enlightened the bleak dark
A smile tugged at my heart
As I basked in the epiphany

You and me cannot be a coincidence

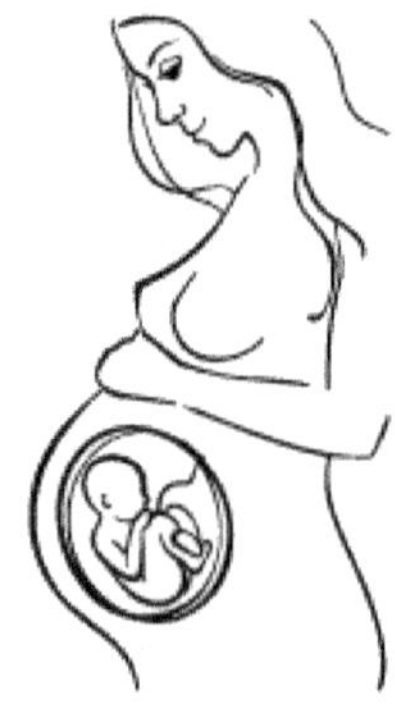

You and me, cannot be a coincidence
Our energies gravitating to coincide
I am sure you have chosen to oblige
At this favourable time

To remind me to pause and reflect
To acknowledge the miracle of life
To cherish my blessings
To help me rediscover and realign

I know my life is going to change
Everything I planned may have to be shelved

But I know for sure your efforts are not in vain
There is something in store that is just right

I promise not to ignore
Every unsaid message
Awakening my inside
And relent control to let you drive

The Prayer

Gratitude O mighty universe for the gift of joy
Joy to behold and reignite my human soul
Joy to feel safe again
And not inherit my insecurities
Joy to be strong again
And not be a coward owing to my fears
Joy to be objective again
And not be clouded with prejudice
Joy to be mindful again
And not be muddled with presumptions
Joy to be confident again
And not be influenced by the choices of others
Joy to follow the dreams again
And not be burdened by aspirations
Joy to be my own person again
And not look for validation
Joy to own the action again
And not find an excuse in redemption
Joy to be happy again

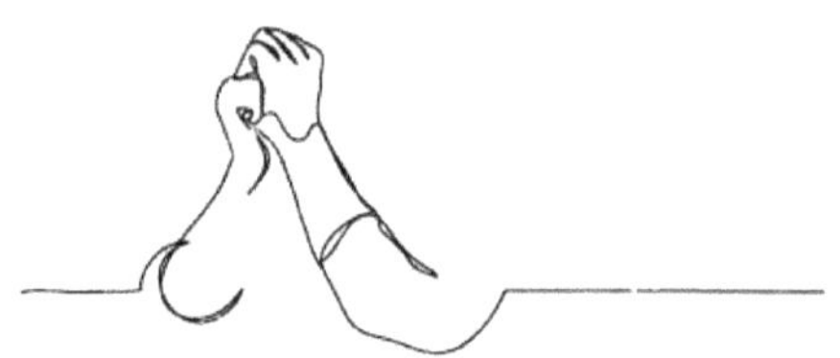

Just know you are enough for your life

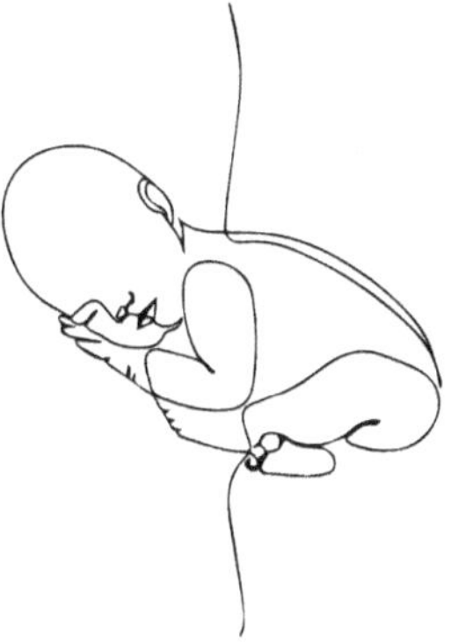

Till yesterday, I spent every moment To find the person responsible for my life
I blamed my dad
For forcing me to select the profession of his choice
I blamed my mom
For equipping me with skills valuable for the life of her time
I blamed my sister
For forcing me to be always by her side
I blamed my brother
For forcing me to return home in time

Till yesterday, you did not come into my life

As I hold you in my arms today

My heart sings a tune of a different kind
I find myself outdated, yet relevant
I can only advise based on my past life
I can only care based on how I have learnt
I can only teach based on what I know

So, today I apologise in advance
For any pain I may cause
But know deep down
That I have only your best interest at heart
So, when I push my thought
Don't feel you have no choice…

Just know you are enough for your life

I await to share with you the magic of my world

I await to share with you the magic of my world
Where we will tirelessly chase the ants for fun
Aimlessly flitting like the butterflies
Make acquaintance with the buds
Be awed by the earthworms
And follow their crusade to till the world
Stay intently focused to trap a housefly
Only to be happily defeated without a grudge
Promise to make a hovercraft
Mimicking a dragonfly
Watch the fireflies
Mesmerizingly glow in the dark
Climb the trees to find the places
Where squirrels hide their nuts
The Ghostly star light stories will keep the
nights up
And chasing the soft feathery fudges
Will never cease to be our favourite fun

I await eagerly, so we can together
Discover some more magical parts of this world

Gift of Love

When I first held you in my arms
I made a promise
To shower you with love

With love I comforted you to sleep
And made sure you ensured I was at peace

With love I cooked you a healthy meal
And made sure you had gratitude for the hands
that made the meal

With love I paid attention to all your needs
And made sure you learned honesty is all I heed

With love I encouraged you to explore the
natural world
And made sure you were at peace with the
harmony

With love I narrated the stories of human
perseverance
And made sure your heart was filled with
reverence

With love I never condemned your new-age
thoughts
And made sure you accepted where I came from

With love I packed your dreams with my dreams
And made sure you never forgot my bucket list

With love I forgave your misdeeds
And made sure you embraced my fallacies

With love I battled your raging storms
And made sure you are aware of how I feel

With love I taught you how to love
For love to stay a home for ease, comfort and
safety

With love I taught you how to love
For love to preside naturally

With love I taught you how to love
For love to continue to be the deep eternal
connection

Respect - Please show me how

I wanted to walk, you lifted me up
Was that respect or was I a little slow

I was not hungry, you forced me to eat
Was that respect or you simply didn't trust

I wanted to scribble, you forced me to colour
Was that respect or you thought I didn't know

I wanted to wear red, you made me wear blue
Was that respect or you thought I didn't look good

I wanted to serve you but you stopped me to
Was that respect or you thought I wouldn't be able to

I wanted to ask but you answered first
Was that respect or you thought I didn't have
words

Respect, if now I can't accept
Respect, if now I can't trust
Respect, if now I can't judge
Respect, if now I can't tolerate
Respect, if now I can't feel good
Respect, if now I can't wait
Respect, if now I can't express

Respect - Please show me how

I lost my cool

I saw your friend write better than you
I lost my cool and wondered should I work on
you
I saw your friend speak better than you
I lost my cool and wondered should I work on
you
I saw your friend read better than you
I lost my cool and wondered should I work on
you
I saw your friend score better than you
I lost my cool and wondered should I work on
you
I saw your friend run better than you
I lost my cool and wondered should I work on
you
I saw your friend draw better than you
I lost my cool and wondered should I work on
you

I saw your friend sing better than you
I lost my cool and wondered should I work on
you
I saw genius, smart and intelligent
I lost my cool and wondered should I work on
you
Then I saw the magic of a child in you
I am glad, even if I lost my cool
I did not cure you of you

Rest assured I will learn

Don't worry about teaching me
Rest assured I will learn.

The first time I departed from your care
Was my first day in this world.

The fluids drained
My lungs inflated
I took my first breath

And Oh! I survived in this world

That was when, the first lesson I learnt

Observe the environment
Heed to my senses
Care to act

And above all, simply stay humble

Reflection

One day someone said,
You are so cute!
You are an exact reflection of mine!

I couldn't stop myself but feel the pride
Accepted the compliment, with an end-to-end
smile

On another day someone said,
You are so stubborn as a mule!

I lowered my head and walked away
Hoping no one would claim You are an exact
reflection of mine!

I have to be the best of "ME"

When you were four your teacher asked,
What would you like to be?
With no hesitation you said it all,
My mom is all I want to be

I want to speak like her...
I want to dress like her...
I want to cook like her...
I want to care like her…
I want to dance like her…
I want to sing like her…
I want to think like her…
I want to work like her...
I want to grace like her...
I want to be kind like her......

A tear rolled and set my goal
All I have to do is just be the best of 'ME'!

My choice is only you

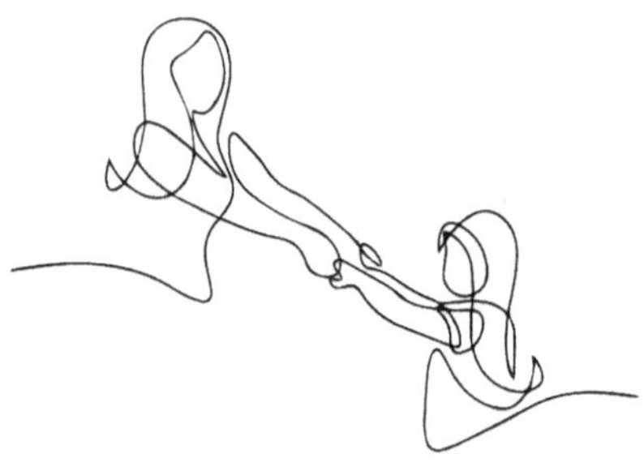

To salvage my pride or to wreck my identity
To fight for dignity or to suffer in obscurity
To act in hope or stay inert unnoticed
To take responsibility or to cower in excuses
To give a chance or disregard self-worth
To climb, catch the light or slide into the
trenches

Standing at crossroads
Waiting for a compromise
Between my charging heart
And my calculating mind
I caught a sight
For there lay the obvious choice
Never to deprive,
You my child of the possibility

You stood there solemn
And I announced to me

"My choice is only you"

Both my heart and my mind, finally
synchronized
To fight together, on the same side

My heart knows nothing but just love

When I was asleep
I had a dream
The touch, the feel, my thumb in your grasp
I knew that I would never be left
I squeezed my eyes tightly shut
The dream may break a little scared....

The breath came warm on my cheek
The sound was like a sweet melody
You my mom sang to me....
You my mom sang to me
First time ever in my dream
You my mom sang to me...

My heart knows nothing but just love

My heart knows nothing but just love
Oh my sweet little angel, open your eyes
Look around fear not I stand near...

I walked, I ran, took the strides
Seldom small often wide
My heart knew nothing but your love

I would slip you would smile
I would fall you stood tall
I would cry you would frown
I would lose you would win

I would fear you had let go......

I squeezed my eyes tightly shut
The dream may break a little scared....
The breath came warm on my cheek
The sound was like a sweet melody

My heart knows nothing but just love

My heart knows nothing but just love
Oh my sweet little angel, open your eyes
Look around fear not I stand near...

I would glide you would laugh
I would rise you felt satisfied
I would smile wipe your frown
I would win you would pride

Now my eyes saw the dream
They didn't need to squeeze to shut

My heart sang all the time
The sound was like a sweet melody

My heart knows nothing but your love
Every time I open my eyes
I know you are standing near
And I see nothing that I fear
Mom! My heart knows nothing but your love…..
My heart knows nothing but your love…..

Legacy together

You and I have some serious work to do
We have to build a legacy together

We will collect some old golds
And add some new gems
To create an inheritance
For peace to transcend generations

I will learn to be naive
You be a little mature
With every setback
We will promise to grow
Rising from the ashes
We will build a stronger self tomorrow

Eyeing something that was not his
Even brought the mighty Ravan to his knees
I intend to pass to you the rich cultural heritage
of human stories
For you to challenge and for me to reflect

So we continue to adopt and adapt
Moralities that keep humanity safe

We will explore the world together
To feel the heat and the chill
To feel the hard and the soft
To feel the friction and the harmony
To feel the turbulence and the symphony
So that these etch in our memory
And empathise the journey of being

We will walk the path hand in hand
Value the love that makes us human
With a hand to break the fall
We can all dare to dream on.

Another Chance

My Heavens, you seem to be cheerful today
With tuffs of happiness floating by

Did you seem a little down yesterday?
I don't remember checking on the blank skies.

Or is it that I turned a blind eye?
In the fear, you may cry...
In the fear, I may have to lend my time...

Today, in your happiness, I find my solace
Assuming you have come out strong

But deep down I know...
I know I have missed the moment

And only pray you will find it in you to let me in
again!

The Custard Apple

This morning, again, I was rushing by
And all of a sudden you caught my eye
Hanging solo from a branch
You brought me to a sudden halt
Standing there I sensed a loss
How did I miss you bud?
Wish I had....
Relished your fragrance
Wish I had....
Appreciated your infant potential
Wish I had....
Admired your growing spirit
Today as I see you ready
Ripe to embrace your destiny
I am left with a nagging thought
Would it have been different?
If only I had slowed down…

My wish for thee

Words betray me
Every time, I try to make a wish for thee

I wish friends for thee
But I am not sure who you would like as
company

I wish a lucrative job for thee
But I am not sure who you would like to be

I wish a big house for thee
But I am not sure how you would like to live

I wish a family for thee
But I am not sure what your dream would be

So I try my best to just stay honest
As I wish you a life you desire to be

So I try my best to cheer you on
As I wish you have courage to pursue your
dreams

So I try my best to be a ray of hope
As I wish you can find light when you feel low

So I try my best to cherish you always
As I wish you can discover "the magic of thee"

I trust you the most with your life

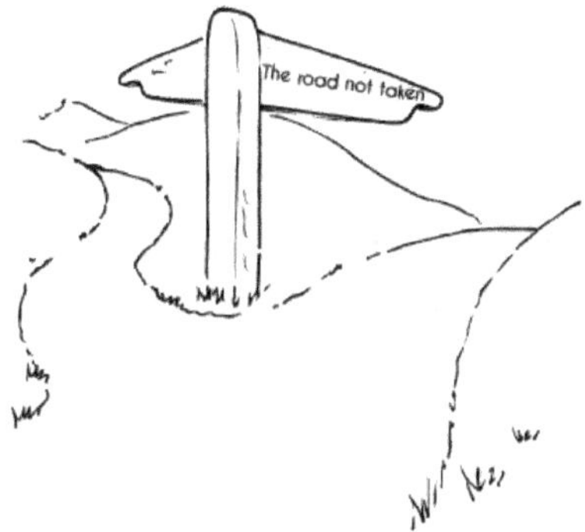

I trust you the most with your life
I trust myself to be just your guide
I trust you to seek help when you like
I trust myself to be there right by your side
I trust you will take the first step, in time
I trust myself to cheer you from the sideline
I trust you will speak when you have your voice
I trust myself to lend you my ear and time
I trust your opinions will be based on your
experience
I trust myself to nudge you into reflection
I trust your conviction will be built by
exploration
I trust myself to challenge your actions
I trust you will discover your passion

I trust myself to watch on with elation
I trust you will uncover your path
I trust myself to never doubt your direction
I trust occasionally you will falter and fail
I trust myself to encourage you to rise and start
over again
I trust you will write your own story
I trust myself to read it objectively
I trust you will find contentment
I trust myself to celebrate my satisfaction